CAMPING OUT

by REBECCA ANDERS   pictures by G. OVERLIE

Lerner Publications Company • Minneapolis, Minnesota

LIBRARY OF CONGRESS CATALOGING IN PUBLICATION DATA

Anders, Rebecca.
Camping out.

(An Early Craft Book)
SUMMARY: Provides information about camping, such as
necessary clothing, camp sites, cooking outdoors, and what to
do if you get lost.

1. Camping—Juvenile literature. [1. Camping] I. Overlie,
George. II. Title.

GV191.7.A53 1976   796.54   76-12059
ISBN 0-8225-0886-9

International Standard Book Number: 0-8225-0886-9
Library of Congress Catalog Card Number: 76-12059

2 3 4 5 6 7 8 9 10 85 84 83 82 81 80 79

Contents

Long ago

In 1603, a French explorer named Samuel de Champlain watched in amazement as two Indian paddlers in a sleek bark boat glided swiftly across a lake. The Indians "made holes" with their paddles in the deep blue Canadian water, pushing themselves along with powerful, rhythmic strokes.

The early French explorers and fur traders soon learned that the fastest and best way to cross North America was to adapt the Indians' bark boat to their needs. This boat they called the *canot* (kah-NO), or, in English, the canoe. By 1700 so many people were paddling canoes into the wilderness that special canoe factories had to be built around Montreal.

Deep in the forests, the Indians would paddle their loads of furs into Hudson Bay Company outposts to trade for supplies brought in by the French traders. The Indians, traders, and trappers often paddled and camped out for months

before reaching an outpost. And their months in the wilderness usually were filled with bone-chilling weather and lean diets. But the Indians and explorers knew how to live off the land—they depended on the wilderness for their food, transportation, and daily living.

Today most people camp in the woods to be near nature. They want to enjoy the tingling freshness of outdoors air and see wild animals in their natural homes. Some people take camping vacations because they want to "rough it" just the way the Indians and early explorers did. For these reasons, three of my friends and I decided to live in the wilderness for a few days.

Canoeing and backpacking into the woods— that's what we had been dreaming about for months. We wanted to feel the sticky pitch of pine under our fingernails and "make holes" with canoe paddles in the sparkling blue-grey of the Canadian Boundary Waters. We dreamed of evening campfires and snug pine-needle beds, never giving thought to "no-see-ums" (tiny biting insects), aching muscles, and unwashed bodies.

Our destination was Gun Lake, a rocky pool of cold water and walleyed pike, and the last lake in a chain of seven. But, with our poorly packed 40-pound backpacks, we made only three portages (carrying canoes overland) and three lakes the first day. The wind blew against us all afternoon, and the "holes" we made with our paddles were lost in the choppy water. We would paddle three strokes forward and be blown two strokes backward.

That first day of backpacking and portaging made us realize what hard work "roughing it" really is. Like true greenhorns, we had to hang packs off our fronts as well as our backs to keep from tipping over. The 80-pound canoes, however, were easy to carry, because weight borne on the head is easier to balance. The worst thing that could happen to a canoe being carried overhead was that it would bump against a rock and boom like thunder, giving

the portager sore ears and a headache.

Our last portage was so long that we had to unload our canoes on land. They looked as clumsy as swans out of water. While we rested, we could only stare at each other weakly as we nursed wounded fingers and wiped away sweat with our red bandannas. Sprawled on the moss and rock trail, we stared up at the birch trees fluttering their little fan-leaves in the sun.

Through the leaves we saw a bush pilot fly over with the cabin of his aquaplane full of lazy greenhorns and his pontoons loaded with canoes. We sighed, shook our heads, and shouldered the packs and canoes once again, for we were determined to see nature close-up.

We portaged and paddled and fought the wind so much that afternoon that we had to give up our struggle on a rocky island halfway across Fairy Lake, the third lake in our chain.

The island campsite looked so inviting that we could hardly wait to pitch our tent and get a roaring fire going. We paced off our little island, assuring ourselves that no bear would bother to swim so far for the stew we planned to eat in an hour. We were as hungry as the timber wolves that howl at the icy northern Minnesota winters.

After supper we ran down to the water's edge to rinse off the plates and wash the day's grime from our faces. The nip of the water and the chilly night air drove us early to our sleeping bags. We nestled into our spiny bed of rock and sand as if it were feather ticking. The last thing I remember before falling asleep was the fog swirling off the lake. It danced and played under the slice of moon like a fairy made of mist.

The next morning I woke to the long throaty cry of a loon hunting for its breakfast. Shaking the pine needles from my hair, I noticed how stiff my neck muscles were. They ached, but hunger drove me out of bed. My friends and I stirred up a batch of flapjacks and gobbled them down in no time. Little did we dream that three days later, on Gun Lake, a bear would devour

our breakfast before we had a chance to taste it. We would watch, open-mouthed and hungry, as it trotted into the woods with our last flapjack.

Planning your trip

If you enjoy the outdoors and want to have your own adventures in the woods, you should start preparations now. First, decide where you want to go. In planning your trip, write to both state and national park services for information on trails and campsites. Be sure to ask for reliable maps, which you should study before setting out on your trip.

Then try camping out in your backyard or somewhere near your home. Even if you can't cook out, you can at least find out what it's like to curl up under the stars with a friend or two and tell ghost stories or sing camp songs. After you have braved a night or two in your own backyard, you are ready to begin packing for your trip.

What to take and how to pack it

Of course, you won't want to take everything you own on your camping trip. In fact, you may have to decide what things you can do without, such as a pillow or an air mattress.

But, when you pack your knapsack or backpack, you must include the essentials for daily living: clothing, food, cooking utensils, bedding, a few tools, and a small first aid kit. Make a list of items you'll need for the wilderness *before* you begin packing. A simple list would look like this:

> bedding (sleeping bag or bedroll)
>
> cooking and eating utensils (pots, pans, plates, cups, knives, forks, spoons, and a can opener)
>
> first aid kit (with aspirin, antiseptic, bandages, tape, lip balm, and sun-tan lotion)
>
> flashlight (with the lens taped in cellophane tape so that it will not shatter if dropped)

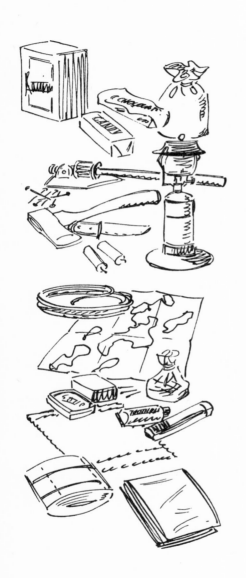

food (You will need about a pound of food a day for young people and a pound and a half a day for adults. Be sure to include high-energy candy as pocket snacks.)

knife, hatchet, small shovel, rope, and a few nails

lantern or candles

map (Be sure you and your friends have traced out your exact route on a map before you leave, and let somebody at home know exactly where you are going.)

matches (Waterproof an emergency supply of matches by dipping them in melted wax, letting them cool before you store them in a plastic bag.)

personal items (soap, the kind that floats so you won't lose it at the bottom of a lake or stream, and a washcloth, toothbrush, and toothpaste)

plastic bags (These are for packing your garbage. Never bury the garbage you can't burn. Take it with you.)

toilet paper (the white kind, because

dyes in colored paper hurt the environ-
ment)

water purifying kit.

These are only the essentials. You may want
to include a camera, binoculars, fishing tackle,
or a fancy tent. But you must decide how heavy
a backpack you will feel comfortable carrying.
If your pack makes you huff and sweat after
only five minutes on the trail, it is too heavy for
you. You don't want to make yourself so tired
that you miss the wonders around you.

For a more comfortable hike with your backpack, put soft items of clothing near the back of
the pack in order to pad your backbone. If
possible, place the heaviest part of the load
toward the top of the pack—this will make
balancing easier. Put your personal items—
soap and toilet paper—in a little bag that can
be reached easily. Tie all the items you may
need along the trail to your belt loops or to
the pack.

Light-weight but warm sleeping bags filled

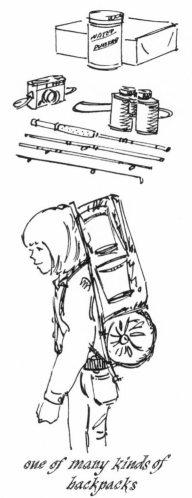

one of many kinds of
backpacks

with fluffy goose down are well worth the money. A down bag can be rolled or jammed into almost any small space for carrying. And it "breathes," allowing body moisture to escape while you are sleeping in it.

Trail clothes

Camping duds should be loose-fitting and comfortable rather than fashionable. They should protect you from wind, rain, and sun. You will need strong, durable clothing that can take the punishment of rugged outdoor living.

Three things you probably thought you'd never need out in the woods, especially in the middle of summer, are a hat, gloves, and a bandanna. The hat will keep the hot sun off your head and neck and will protect your head from pesky mosquitoes and deer flies. You can wear the bandanna as a sweat-band around your neck, use it as a washcloth, make it into an emergency pot holder, or wave it as a signal for help. Most bandannas are red, a good color to wear camping because it makes you stand out from the deep greens and browns of the forest. However you dress for hiking, be sure that you wear bright colors at all times. You don't want a hunter to mistake you for a deer!

A pair of gloves may make your hands warm and sticky in the summer, but gloves will save your skin from being nicked and bruised while you are loading your pack, making camp, or breaking off sticks for firewood.

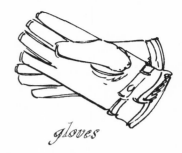

gloves

Since your feet will be doing the hardest work, shoes are the most important item of clothing. You will need a good pair of thick-soled shoes or hiking boots that support the ankles and protect the feet from rocks and twigs.

hiking boots

Pamper your feet while hiking. Trim the toe-nails straight across to avoid painful ingrown nails, and wear two pairs of socks in your boots to cushion your feet—the pair of socks next to your skin should be turned inside out so that the little yarn balls and knots won't rub against

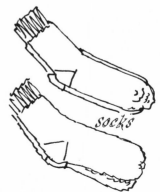

socks

the feet, creating blisters. Use talcum powder to prevent chafing on your feet or on any other part of your body that feels hot and itchy.

Make a clothing checklist before you leave for the woods:

a comfortable pair of jeans or loose-fitting pants

a bright-colored long-sleeved shirt or jacket

a cap or hat, bandanna, and gloves (The cap can double as a night-cap, should the air get frosty.)

a change of socks and underwear (You can wash your dirty socks and underwear and hang them on your pack to dry while you hike.)

a sweater (that you can wear to bed for extra warmth or use as a pillow or nightcap)

a waterproof poncho (This loose-hanging garment will cover you and your pack when it rains. Or use it to cover your firewood at night, or spread it on the ground under your sleeping bag.)

Walking like an Indian

To be a good hiker and to keep from tiring yourself, you may have to learn to walk all over again! Instead of bobbing along the sidewalk like the city dweller, heel first, the woods Indian floats along the forest floor with feet pointed straight or turned slightly inward to keep from tripping over tree roots or rocks. For good balance, the forest walker lands with the foot level, or the weight shifted slightly towards the ball of the foot. This slightly forward motion enables the hiker to keep up momentum, which saves time and energy.

With each step you take in the woods, you will land on something different. But you should be prepared for it if you scan the trail ahead for slippery moss-covered rocks, holes, or over-hanging branches. Train your eyes to tell your feet how to walk and where.

Take a five-minute rest every hour. Should you huff and puff over a steep trail and rest for

rest 5 minutes every hour

half an hour, your hard-working muscles will cool off and shorten, giving you a sore and crampy feeling when you get up to hike again.

As you get more camping experience, you will learn to be a pessimist about two things: how early in the morning you can break camp and how far you can travel the next day. Most young hikers overestimate their abilities.

Picking a campsite

If you have been canoeing or hiking all day, you will probably be so weary by late afternoon that any campsite will do. But if you don't take care to pick a good site, you may spend an uncomfortable night in a windblown or marshy spot with pebbles and clumps of brush for a bed. To avoid a night of tossing and turning, look for level, dry ground free of rocks and holes. Make sure that there is a nearby source of drinking water (which you can purify with a special water-purifying kit or by boiling for five minutes). Look around for dry firewood close to your site and stones with which to make a fireplace.

When you are choosing a campsite, avoid swampy areas full of stagnant water. These areas are likely to breed mosquitoes in such abundance that you will be up all night slapping and scratching.

Avoid patches of poison ivy, poison oak, or poison sumac. If you think you have touched any of these plants, wash the affected skin with lots of sudsy soap and water.

Be especially careful to avoid these plants when you choose a spot for an outdoor toilet. Dig your "whoopee hole" behind some bushes about 30 feet from your campsite (and be sure to cover it up before you leave the area).

Look for

water source

plenty of firewood

Avoid

poison oak

poison sumac

poison ivy

Building a fire

Campfires are cheerful, cozy, and warm. But, more importantly, they cook your food.

To have a fire, you must have a fireplace. The simplest kind of fireplace is built out of a ring of rocks. Scrape away leaves and twigs until you reach bare ground. Then place a ring of rocks, about five feet (one and one half meters) in diameter, around the cleared area.

To build a good cooking fireplace, you will need to find flat rocks that you can overlap to make two walls facing each other. Make a third wall, either by piling more rocks together or by using the side of a ledge as a wall. This kind of fireplace will funnel the heat up to the pans placed over the gap between the two facing walls. Cooking fires are best if the fire is small and the heat is concentrated.

To make a fire, you will need three kinds of wood: tinder, kindling, and fuel wood. Tinder is fine-textured dry material that catches the

2 kinds of fireplaces

simple fireplace

cooking fireplace

make gap narrow so pans can sit over it

flame from your match to start the main fire. Facial tissue, wax paper, dry leaves, bark, wood shavings, and dry pine needles all make good tinder. Tinder is quick-burning.

Kindling is finger-sized wood that carries the flame to the fuel wood, or logs. A dead tree left standing is a good source of kindling.

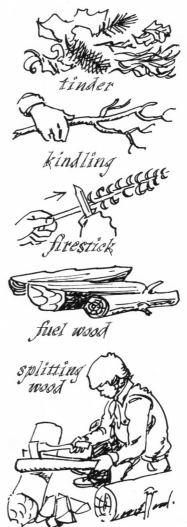

tinder

kindling

firestick

fuel wood

splitting wood

Firesticks, a combination of tinder and kindling, can be whittled from pine twigs. With a knife (blade pointed away from you!), make wispy curlicues out of the bark on the twig. These dry bark curlicues will quickly feed the licking flames. Two or three firesticks together should start a brisk blaze.

Fuel wood is the bulkiest of the three woods. Because it burns for the longest time, it does the cooking. If fuel wood is not provided at your campsite, use standing deadwood or dried-out driftwood, which can be found along the shore of a lake. Ask an older friend who knows how to use an ax to help split your firewood. Split logs burn better than whole ones.

A word of warning: *never* pour gasoline or kerosene onto your fire to get it going. You could burn yourself seriously.

When you start a fire in the woods, it is your job to see that it is completely out when you are done with it. Leaving a fireplace with even slightly warm ashes is inviting trouble. Forest fires are usually started by careless people who never intended to cause millions of dollars of damage and the deaths of thousands of animals.

To drown your fire, pour water on it, turning over each charred stick or log to make sure its underside is doused, too. Pour on more water; then stir the ashes. Repeat this process until the ashes are floating and cold to the touch. Drown your fire with as many buckets of water as it takes to give you peace of mind.

Outdoors cooking

Food cooked over an open fire will taste good whether it turns out according to recipe or not.

DROWN *your fire!*

Toting packs up and down trails and breathing pine-scented fresh air will give you such an appetite that even peanut butter and jelly sandwiches with a little trail sand in them will taste good.

freeze-dried foods

But there are a few secrets to outdoor cooking you should know before you go camping. When you grocery shop, look for items with "instant" or "minute" on the package. These kinds of packaged foods have had the water taken out of them and will be lighter in your packs than regular canned food.

Green sticks on which you have whittled sharp points are good for toasting and broiling. You can toast bread, bacon, hot dogs, and marshmallows on sticks held over a low fire or hot embers.

Shmoors are a quick-energy snack made from toasted marshmallows, graham crackers, and chocolate bars. All you have to do is toast your marshmallow to a golden brown and put it on a

~ Shmoors ~

wrap ~ bake 15 minutes

embers ~ no flame

chocolate bar laid between two graham crackers. The hot marshmallow will melt the chocolate into a delicious gooey mass.

Another nourishing, quick-energy snack can be made from canned peaches. Simply drain the peaches, place a marshmallow in the hollow of each peach half, sprinkle the peaches with brown sugar, and wrap them individually in aluminum foil. Place them on hot embers for 10 to 15 minutes. Then, take them out of the fire with a stick, open them up, and enjoy a syrupy, fragrant treat.

Potatoes in their jackets can be baked directly in the fire. Simply wait for the first burst of flame to die down and, when the embers are hot, place your potatoes on them. Bake for two hours, remove from the coals, scrape as much of the charcoal off the skins as you can, and eat them with salt and pepper.

Alphabet stew is another easy dish to prepare. Simply brown a pound and a half of hamburger in your fry pan, pour in two cans of alphabet noodle soup, stir, and let simmer for 15 minutes. There should be enough stew for four people. (Fresh meat will not keep long, so this is a good dish with which to treat yourself on your first night out.)

Flapjacks are good for either breakfast or supper. To make a simple but hearty batch, you will need:

> 1/2 quart flour
> 1/2 teaspoon of salt
> 1 teaspoon of sugar
> 1 level tablespoon of baking powder
> dehydrated milk (to which you will add water).

Add milk to the dry ingredients until the batter is slightly runny. Spoon it in silver-dollar sized portions into a hot greased frying pan. Fry the flapjacks to a golden brown on each side. Top with honey, jam, or syrup.

To the beginning camp cook, frying directly over the flames seems like a good idea. But it can be dangerous because the grease in the pan

~ *Flapjacks* ~

add water to dehydrated milk

add milk to dry ingredients ~ mix

spoon into a hot greased pan

fry golden brown on each side

Serve!

fire reduced to coals

is likely to catch fire. You should, instead, wait for the flames to die down and fry over a bed of hot coals. The heat will be more constant this way.

If you should catch a fish

Unlike the early French trappers who caught their dinners, you shouldn't depend on living off the land. If you do catch a fish, though, you will enjoy one of the tastiest outdoor meals ever.

Live bait won't be hard to find. Simply dig for earthworms and grubs. Push your bait onto the fish hook lengthwise so a fish won't make off with the juicy tail of the worm without biting the hook.

push bait on hook lengthwise

If you catch a pike or a crappie, put it on a stringer in the water until you are ready to clean it. A stringer is a thin rope with a sharp metal point that you will push through the mouth of the fish and out the gills. The stringer in water will keep your catch alive and fresh until you are ready to kill it and clean it. When you take your fish out of the water, give it a hard blow on the head.

Now you are ready to scale your fish. A scaler is an inexpensive little tool with teeth on it that will remove the inedible scales from the fish's skin. Grab your fish by the tail and scale it from tail to head. Rinse it in clean water.

Have a grown-up friend help you remove the head of the fish just behind the gills with a sharp knife. Then cut out the dorsal fin (the fin on the fish's back) and the tail. Carefully slit the belly lengthwise and remove the insides. Rinse again. Keep the fish in cool water in the shade until you are ready to fry it.

To cook your fish, take it out of its bath and roll it in a one to one mixture of flour and cornmeal. Fry it in a hot greased pan until it turns a golden brown on both sides. Don't forget to salt it!

fish on stringer

scaler

dorsal fin · cut
cut →
head removed
slit belly

remove insides—
rinse fish in water—
fry in hot pan

Bedding down for the night

clear sleeping area of stones and twigs

level off area

make hip hole

ground

Before you bed down for a night of campfire conversation and deep dozing, clear your sleeping area of pebbles and twigs. Tiny stones under a tent floor can turn into boulders of discomfort overnight, and mere twigs will seem like logs. Make sure, too, that the ground on which you are bedding down is level. Nothing feels worse than having all the blood rush to your head while you are trying to sleep.

Since most people are heaviest through their hips, it is a good idea to dig a hip hole under your sleeping bag or tent floor. Shape a little basin of earth so that it molds to your bottom. By doing this, you will make a comfortable bed for yourself and won't have to bother toting an air-mattress and blowing it up every night.

A good pillow can be made out of your rolled-up trail clothes stuffed into a T-shirt. In the morning, pull your clothes into the sleeping bag with you to warm them up before putting them on.

If you aren't sound asleep by sundown, you may need a source of light other than your campfire. You can either buy gasoline lanterns or make candle lanterns. To make a candle lantern, simply snip out a "window" in a tin can, leaving the can lid attached in one place to make a handle. Run the bottom of a candle through a flame once or twice so that the wax is soft, and push the softened end into the bottom of the tin-can holder. You can nail the lid of the can to a log or stump. Remember to nail your light to the side away from the wind.

Before you blow out your lantern, go down your good-night check-list. You should check:

food (Make sure that all your food is wrapped and out of the reach of animals. With a rope, sling your food pack from a high tree limb.)

fuel (Make sure that it is covered and that you have enough cut for breakfast.)

Tin-can lantern
← wind
stump

Good-night check-list
1 ←food
2
firewood covered

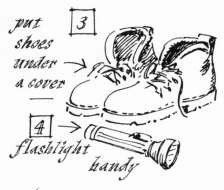

put
shoes
under →
a cover
———

flashlight
handy

shoes (Put them under cover for the night. Nothing feels worse in the morning than a damp shoe with bugs in it.)

flashlight (should be within reach if you have to go out in the middle of the night).

What to do if you get lost

Never, for any reason, leave the group with which you are camping. But, if you should be separated from your friends, sit down and force yourself to be calm. This will keep you from panicking and losing yourself deeper in the woods.

If you don't know the direction from which you came and, therefore, can't backtrack, stay where you are. Try building a large smoky fire to attract the attention of forest rangers. The more greenery you toss on your fire, the smokier it will be.

If, without traveling too far, you see a high point of ground, go stand on it and look for familiar landmarks. A good hiker always notices a few landmarks along the trail and tucks them away for future reference.

Don't worry about food, for you can go almost a week without it; but do eat the snacks you have stuffed into your pockets *sparingly*.

Always check in with the local park service before you go camping, so that if you should get lost, people will know roughly where to look for you.

Wild animal watching

By stepping out of your comfortable life into the wilderness, you will have the opportunity of watching animals in their natural homes. If you are lucky, a deer may surprise you one night, its large chocolate eyes drawn by the brightness of your campfire; or a raccoon may scuttle across your campsite in search of food. Or, while hiking, you may see a mother quail hobbling in front of you with her wing dangling, pretending to be injured in order to draw you away from her babies.

Whatever your reason for going into the wilderness, remember that you are a guest there. If you and your friends learn to take care of the outdoors, you can enjoy camping and animal-watching again and again.